Ramsey

The Power Of The Human-Canine Bond;
Turning Your Passion Into A Business

Chris Kent & Marie Yates

Published by Love Learning from Dogs Publishing House

First Published by Love Learning from Dogs Publishing House

Text copyright: Chris Kent and Marie Yates 2017

ISBN: 978-0-9957365-0-4

Cover picture: Andy David Wright (www.andydavidwright.com)

Contents

Foreword

Fortunately for dogs, and us, awareness of the extraordinary ways in which canines can enrich human lives continues to grow. As someone who has the good fortune to work full time with animals I know how beneficial a relationship with a four-legged companion can be.

I am often contacted by like-minded people looking to make their dreams a reality and receive many messages and emails containing questions along the lines of; *'How can I utilise the relationship I have with my dog to help others?' 'My dog has changed my life; how do you recommend I start a project to help other people discover this sense of companionship and joy?' "My rescue dog rescued me. What do I need to do to develop a business that will help other people and dogs in need?'* Questions I have not been able to answer fully, until now.

When I was asked to write this forward not only was I honoured, as I have great admiration for Chris Kent and Marie Yates, but I was excited too as it gave me the opportunity to learn more about their inspiring work. Although I interact with dogs in many capacities, and of course all dogs are extraordinary teachers and facilitators, the field of Canine Partnership for Personal Development is not my area of expertise. As well as giving me plenty of food for thought this publication has furnished me with the perfect answer to the questions I am frequently asked. From now on my response will be 'read The Power of the Human-Canine Bond'.

Written by Chris Kent from K9 Project and Marie Yates from Canine Perspective CIC, this book is a valuable resource for anyone considering partnering with dogs to empower and support people in any capacity. It is an effortless and highly educational read that guides the reader through all the steps necessary to create a solid foundation on which the business will be built. Based on the authors' own experiences, it offers salient advice exploring the joys and challenges of developing a sustainable and successful business model. It encourages the reader to explore and develop their own ideas, objectives, and goals and contains practical considerations and tips for a successful enterprise with the celebration of dogs, and their wellbeing, at its very core.

Although this book is aimed primarily at those looking to develop a Canine Partnership for Personal Development project, this unique publication fills a gap in the market. It will be of benefit to anyone looking to take that leap of faith and become self-employed or expand an existing business in any animal related enterprise.

Sarah Fisher

(www.tilleyfarm.co.uk)

Introduction

No one appreciates the very special genius of
your conversation as the dog does.
Christopher Morley

Let's start the way we mean to go on, and be totally honest. We're not business experts, we're not here to give you instructions on how to set up and run a business. We're here to share our experiences of running businesses involving dogs and attempting, in our own ways, to offer a means of learning and personal development for humans. We will take you on a journey, inviting you to consider lots of different aspects around starting your business.

We are going to use the term 'business' throughout this book. We'll also be using the term Canine Partnership for Personal Development (CPPD) which is the description that works for us and we hope works for you too. We use the term CPPD 'business' with pride and it's something that might raise an eyebrow or two. Whether you're planning to work in a not-for-profit sector, social enterprise, social business, as a sole trader or limited company, you will only survive by becoming sustainable. There are lots of structures to consider, but we're starting at the beginning so don't worry about that yet. The days of relying totally on funding are gone, and throughout this book we're inviting you to think about your idea in a new way. The more income you can generate, the more people you can work with.

We're two people who have taken our ideas and a huge leap of faith, and made it happen. We've made mistakes and there are things we would have done differently, but they have helped shape where we are now. If we had a pound for every time someone said 'I'd love to do what you do', we'd be millionaires.

Working with dogs to change the lives of humans, a CPPD, is an incredible way to spend our days. If only it was that simple! This book answers the questions that we're regularly asked. It answers those questions in a way that we hope you'll find useful. A lot of the answers you need can only come from you. Yes, you! We have some questions for you that will help you to shape your business, and we invite you to use this book as a way of collating all of your ideas. There are spaces for you to answer questions, and we hope that you'll scribble in all of them. Any ideas that are sparked, write them down. Any lightbulb moments, write them down. At any stage where you think 'I can't do this', be reassured that we have had those moments too. Ok, we said we'd be honest, we still have those moments! When that happens, as it's more likely to be 'when' and not 'if', please bookmark that page, put the book down, go outside and play with your dog!

So, who are 'we'...

Chris Kent

Chris started her working life on adventure playgrounds in the East End of London before training to become a Social Worker. Once qualified she began working in the criminal justice sector with adults and young people experiencing a number of challenges. Throughout her career, Chris has worked in local authorities, charities and not-for-profit organisations, as well as in the private sector.

In 1998, Chris established a successful project development and training consultancy. She worked across local authorities, non-government organisations, and private businesses. In 2008 she combined her extensive experience with her passion for dogs and set up the K9 Project; a canine assisted learning and personal development intervention, working with people of all ages.

The common theme throughout Chris' work initiatives is her passion, motivation, and creativity. With a career that spans four decades she has consistently written, designed and delivered innovative programmes. These programmes encompass a wide variety of expertise, including working with young people to address anger issues, parenting programmes, work based learning for practitioners and professionals, training workshops, and team building events.

Chris has written a book about her journey with the K9 Project. *Hounds Who Heal* is an awe-inspiring story where her creativity, as well as her passion for working with people and her love of animals, all come together.

The K9 Project has supported thousands of people, has won multiple awards and, with Chris at the helm, has blazed a trail for other canine assisted programmes around the world.

Chris is delighted to be co-authoring this book to help other people set up creative, insightful projects with dogs as co facilitators.

Marie Yates

Marie's career started after her graduation from University, where she found her way into working in sports development. She climbed the ranks until she was leading the development of the Paralympic Programme for UK Athletics.

Alongside her work, Marie continued studying and completed a Master's degree, diplomas in personal performance coaching, and decided to follow her passion for writing.

Taking a new role in the Department for Education enabled Marie to develop her project management skills and enhanced her desire to move into self-employment! Marie had been working privately with survivors of sexual violence as coach and mentor, and with her first book being published in 2014, she took the leap.

Marie is the author of *The Dani Moore Trilogy*, a story following the journey of a teenage survivor and her rescue dog. The first book, *Reggie & Me*, reached the final of The People's Book Prize and the books have been endorsed by professionals working in this area.

The trilogy has been the catalyst for establishing Canine Perspective CIC, a social enterprise dedicated to inspiring positive change using the power of the human-canine bond. Marie has gone on to study dog training and behaviour, which has created the synergy within this business. The social projects undertaken include the flagship programme, Canine Hope, which is designed for survivors and incorporates the journey of a canine co-facilitator.

Marie is one of the many people who has been inspired by Chris Kent to follow their dream of working with dogs to create social change. She is excited to be working with Chris to write this book, and can't wait to see the new, innovative projects that will be designed to make a positive change.

Working Together

We decided to write this book together as we have taken completely different approaches to running our businesses. We have different legal structures, there have been structural changes, and our motivation is different. We work with different client groups, and we work in different ways. We know that there isn't one answer, and we believe that this collaborative approach will offer you a wider range of questions to help you as you embark upon this journey. We have also called upon other people who are running businesses, working with dogs and humans, so you can enjoy words of wisdom from people who have been there and are doing this.

The book follows a logical approach. It starts with your idea and we invite you to follow the process and develop your idea as you would an excitable puppy. Bouncing around, embracing your ideas like falling autumn leaves is fun, but you won't be catching anything. The adolescent phase will potentially hit you at some point. Allow yourself to forget everything you've learnt, to have a tantrum if you need to, and then, as the fog starts to lift, your business puppy will really start to take shape. It will become reliable and consistent in its development and then, you'll have the solid foundation on which to build.

Enjoy!

Chapter One: How Does a Canine Partnership for Personal Development Work?

No matter how little money and how few possessions you own, having a dog makes you rich.

Louis Sabin

It may be that you have arrived at the point of wanting to work with dogs and people from a 'dog perspective' first. Are you an experienced dog guardian/trainer/behaviourist and want to use this expertise to help people, too? Or maybe you are a 'people' professional first and you already work with people in a therapeutic/ support/educational or personal development setting, and want to add dogs to your range of services – because you know how awesome they can be.

Either way, for this section we wanted to talk about how and why dogs are such powerful facilitators of change, as well as discussing how we all learn, and some of the key theories we believe will help you to work within the field of CPPD. An ability to form working relationships appropriate to your setting, as well as a sound knowledge of people and dogs, are essential for understanding the processes of helping people make changes in their lives. We apologise if you already know some of this stuff. There's lots more we could have included, but these are varied and collected from a range of sources both in the fields of education, relationship building, and horse and dog training!

We assume you already have some guiding principles to work to; if not, we rather like the solution focussed type approach. It's respectful, person centred and allows for choice.

Guiding Principles

We are all unique and experience the world in different ways.

People respond to their reality, and our perceptions of the world and our experiences within it will not be the same.

Mind and body form a linked system.

When you enable people to feel good within your intervention, you are opening a door to change. As Maya Angelou said "I've learned that people will forget what you said, people will forget what you did, but people will never forget how you made them feel". Of course, the dogs really help with this as they make people feel good, so you are halfway there... at least.

The person you're working with is the expert on their situation.

It doesn't matter how often you see that person or group of people, and let's face it that won't be a whole lot during the course of their week, they are the expert of their situation- not you. This approach ensures you don't dish out advice or guarantees. They will know what's going on.

The person you're working with has all the resources they need to solve their problems.

Sometimes this may seem challenging; remember it's really just your job to help them rediscover, or discover, their own inner resources; after all they have got this far. If you do not believe they can do it, how are you going to help them develop belief in themselves?

What else would you add to personalise the guiding principles that would like to adopt? It's worth thinking about, as they will link to your business vision later on.

Let's get onto talking about the dogs, and why working with dogs is so powerful. After all, it starts and often finishes with them! They are your motivators, your leverage, your starter for 10, your behaviour management tool, your levellers, and of course your canine partners and co-facilitators.

Why work with dogs?

Dogs have a well-documented relationship with humans which can be traced back for thousands of years. From the first steps of co-existence and survival to the forging of intense and mutually beneficial partnerships, dogs now accompany and support us through many of life's challenges and difficulties. What was once a practical arrangement; guarding, moving stock, protection, warmth and the provision of food, has now come, in many societies, to a point where dogs are credited with our survival on an emotional as well as physical level.

Think about the assistance dogs who can put washing in the machine and get the phone when their partners fall out of their wheelchairs. There are seizure alert dogs who can warn their partners when they are going to have a seizure, and there's the relatively new psychiatric assistance dogs who can spot a panic attack coming, and either bring their guardians back to the present moment or guide them back home when they are lost. There are autism support dogs who allow children with autism a new way into the complex world of communication and physical touch. The power of dogs seems to have no limits.

Dogs have walked beside us as we have evolved and developed, and are now a crucial element to emotional wellbeing for many.

There are a raft of studies outlining the therapeutic benefits of dogs (*you can find lots of links on our website*). These include reducing blood pressure, alleviating anxiety, and lifting depression. Living with a dog is credited with giving people healthier hearts, longer lives, and less social isolation. One-off visits to hospitals, schools, nursing homes, and reading centres can trigger happy memories, provide motivation and fun. In otherwise difficult physical therapy sessions, dogs can provide physical contact for those who otherwise may get very little, and encourage reading aloud in a non-critical environment. They make people laugh; one of our dogs dancing on his back legs made a gentleman laugh out loud who had not made a sound for 5 years.

The therapy dog movement is said to have started during World War 2 when member of the 5th Air Force found a tiny Yorkshire Terrier in a fox hole in New Guinea. That's where Corporal Bill Wynne came in, buying her from the person who found her and calling her Smoky. She stayed by his side for 18 months in combat, undertaking daring missions, and being awarded 8 battle stars. When her partner became ill she was taken to visit him in hospital, and Dr Charles Mayo noticed that the wounded soldiers' spirits were lifted greatly when Smoky was around. He allowed her to visit and to sleep in the hospital with her partner. She continued her visits for 12 years. The notion of dogs having a therapeutic benefit is not in question and is something that has immeasurable benefits. What we're doing with CPPD is taking a different approach, working with the dogs and utilising their natural behaviours and abilities to make sustainable changes in people's lives.

So, what is it exactly about dogs that makes them so effective at working alongside us and lifting our spirits? As we will continue to explore, facilitating change not just in moods and attitude, but also in human and canine behaviours. You'll have lots of ideas about this, but here are some of ours.

Dogs are non-judgemental: Dogs really don't care if you are fat or thin, rich or poor, if you can read or write. They do not judge, but they can, and will, give you very clear feedback. We look at examples of this and how you can creatively use this later.

Dogs are often affectionate: It might be that the people you work with are starved of affection. Even if they're not, stroking the dog in a session can lower blood pressure, give you somewhere to hide your face (and emotions!) and provide a distraction.

Dogs live very much in the moment: This is a great tool for discussion. That's not to say they don't remember stuff; but that they do not wallow in it. When they are eating, they are eating; when they are running, they are running. You see the pattern!

Dogs often do like eye contact: Creating the production of oxytocin, the feel good/connection chemical, and therefore filling everyone, including themselves, with a warm feeling of connection. This connection can also help to build trust, something that can be lacking in many of the groups we work with.

Dogs do not lie: If they are fed up, it shows. If they are excited, it shows. They don't lie because they can't; simple. I'm sure if they could, they would (something along the lines of; *'by the way, I haven't had any dinner!'*) However, this is a great aspirational angle to explore trust, communication, role modelling and understanding others.

Dogs help us understand empathy: Sometimes it can be far easier to display empathy for a dog or another animal than fellow human beings. Practising with the dog can lead to discussion and learning about empathy for other people, and seeing things from someone else's perspective.

Dogs don't get embarrassed: Handy!

Now it's your turn.

How will dogs make great additions to the work you would like to do? What will they be teaching the people you're working with?

We talk more in Chapter five about the realities of working with dogs in various environments.

How we learn

We are not going to go into a long scientific definition here, as there are many places that can do that far better than we can. We are just going to talk about learning and change, and how this impacts our work in the field of CPPD.

There is saying in dog training and people training; 'behaviour that is positively reinforced or rewarded gets repeated'. In other words, if it makes you feel good you are more likely to do it again. Simple, right? Except amongst people and dogs, the things that make us feel good are not always the same. Let's take a reward; for one dog, food does it, for another it's retrieving, yet for another dog an encouraging word will suffice. What works best will depend on a blend of factors, genes, breed, environment, previous experiences, age and their current situation. What works at one point in time may eventually need to be changed. It's the same for people. For some, a course certificate is important, while another person may not even choose to take it out of the room. Some people may like to be the employee of the month, while another would cringe with embarrassment. For people who may have their lives impacted by trauma and abuse, their ideas of positive feedback may not be the same as yours. There could be issues around trust, confidence and power. Having said that, if you can make dogs and people feel good, whatever you will be doing will have a greater chance of achieving your aims and objectives. If you know that your idea will enable people and dogs to feel safe and comfortable, then you are at a good starting point.

We also need to remember that our brains are constantly able to change and develop- it is called neuroplasticity – *Wikipedia probably explains it best!*

"Neuroplasticity, also known as brain plasticity or neural plasticity, is an umbrella term that describes lasting change to the brain throughout an individual's life course. The term gained prominence in the latter half of the 20th century, when new research showed that many aspects of the brain can be altered (or are "plastic") even into adulthood. This notion is in contrast with the previous scientific consensus that the brain develops during a critical period in early childhood and then remains relatively unchanged (or "static"). Neuroplasticity can be observed at multiple scales, from microscopic changes in individual neurons to larger-scale changes such as cortical remapping in response to injury. Behaviour, environmental stimuli, thought, and emotions may also cause neuroplastic change through activity-dependent plasticity, which has significant implications for healthy development, learning, memory, and recovery from brain damage."

So, what does that mean for us? Basically, to remember that people can change the way they feel, think and behave. They can actually alter the way their brain functions as a result of some types of training and activities. A true CPPD will enable these changes to take place; that's the power of the work you're going to be doing.

We also need to think about how the mind, the body and the emotions connect. There has long been debate about which comes first, and which is the most successful way to change thought patterns and neural pathways as well as physical states of health. We know that our bodies respond to the way we think, feel, and act. This is one type of 'mind/body connection'. When we are stressed, anxious, or upset, our body reacts in a way that might tell you that something isn't right. There is a general acceptance that psychological and emotional factors can play a role in major illness, and that mind-body techniques can aid in their treatment. In addition, we know that certain types of exercise are not only good for general health, but also releases endorphins which make us feel good. More recent research also indicates that we can change the way our bodies move in order to affect neural pathways for long term change.

In short, the mind/body/emotion link is important, and research indicates that any aspect can 'come first', both in changing behaviour as well as initiating it. This is great news for us, as it means if we can be flexible in our approaches, and let's face it with dogs around you have to be, then we have several opportunities to help behaviour change.

As you're starting to think about how you are going to plan and prepare your sessions in a way that will enable sustainable change and bring in specific learning from your canine co-tutor, we have listed some people-focussed models for you to consider. These are models and theories that we feel are useful for this work. There are many others, and apologies if you're a 'people professional' who already knows these ideas; feel free to make a cuppa and join us again later. All of these models and theories can be explored in greater depth, and we have included some useful links on our website.

Change Theories

Transtheoretical Model of Change

How and why people change their behaviour has been studied from different angles for many years. The transtheoretical model of change is based on 35 years of scientific research, intervention development and scores of empirical studies. The model originally developed by Prochaska and DiClementi incorporates previous theories and identifies 5 stages of change. This is a crucial piece of knowledge if you are in the business of a CPPD business focused on human behaviour change rather than a feel-good visiting scheme.

Precontemplation (not anywhere near ready for change!)

People in the precontemplation stage do not intend to take action in the foreseeable future. They see no reason to; everything is ok as it is! Being un-informed or under-informed about the consequences of behaviour may cause a person to be in the precontemplation stage. Previous unsuccessful attempts at change can lead a person to feel demoralised about their ability to change. Precontemplators are often characterised in other theories as resistant, unmotivated, or unready for help. However, precontemplation is the first stage for everyone who wants to make a change.

Contemplation (getting ready for change!)

Contemplation is the stage in which people intend to change, and they have weighed up the pros and cons of change. This weighing between the costs and benefits of change can produce profound ambivalence that can cause people to remain in this stage for long periods of time. The contemplation stage does not lead to instant action, and people can get stuck here for a while as they continue to consider the things they might need to do in order to get ready for change. So, a contemplator can easily become a procrastinator if they are not helped move forward.

Preparation (I'm ready for change – let's do it)

Preparation is the stage in which people intend to take action in the pretty immediate future. Typically, they have already taken some significant action in the past year. These individuals have a plan of action already at least partly in place and ready to go.

Maintaining the Change (how do I keep this going?)

So, we've changed; now the challenging part of maintaining the change. Support is needed after the initial buzz of achieving change is gone. Strategies are needed to ensure maintenance moves into a new and established behaviour.

Relapse

This is a return to the original behaviour, and is probably temporary. After a rethink of the pros and cons, this lapse is best viewed as a normal 'blip' and as much a stage of the cycle as any other. A chance to review triggers for relapse, create new strategies, and get back on it.

The key for you as a human co-tutor (!) is that you really need to be aware of where a person is on the cycle if you are to keep in step with them. It's pretty pointless talking about strategies for maintaining change if the person you are talking to is a precontemplator. Your task is to help them get to the next stage, whatever that is, one step at a time. The people you'll be working with will usually love this model too as it gives them something to relate to; a shared language and understanding. It also normalises the whole change process.

How will you use this model? Think about the people you're going to be working with, and the situations they are seeking to change. How will you work with a canine co-tutor to help them move through the process?

Comfort Zones

Comfort zones are a great model for both looking at dogs' behaviours and our own human behaviours. We have found this to be a great way of allowing people to discuss their own anxieties in a non-threatening way.

So, a *'comfort zone'* is a zone where you feel completely comfortable, but you'd probably already guessed that! A zone can be a physical place (home/work/school) or people (family/trusted friend) or a location (beach/allotment/shopping centre). Comfort zones can change over time, depending on age, life events and circumstances. The smaller your comfort zone, the less confident you are likely to be. For a dog, this can be displayed as a fear of new places, different floor surfaces, or loud noises; the world can be a scary place for all of us. As responsible dog owners, our task would be to find ways to introduce new things in a calm, kind and positive way, gradually allowing the dog to leave his comfort zone and enter his...

Stretch/learning zone. In the stretch zone, we can just about face doing new things but it is, quite literally, a stretch. We may have to push ourselves to get there. For the scared dog, short periods of walking on different surfaces, exposure gradually to louder noises, all accompanied by positive reinforcement, may enable his comfort zone to include some of the things in his stretch zone. Thus, his comfort zone gets bigger, and learning and growth occur. How can we learn from this as he gets more confident? If he is forced to stay in the stretch zone for too long he may spill over into the...

Panic zone. Nothing can be learnt in the panic zone. The brain is incapable of learning anything new due to the rush of chemicals surging through it. The best bit about a panic zone is that once you are through it and out the other side you can feel relief that you survived it. However, you may also feel so shocked by it you are determined to avoid doing anything similar again. For a dog (or any animal, come to mention it) in the panic zone, nothing good really comes from it. They may shut down due to 'flooding', which may look like acceptance but is really helplessness. As people, we are far better at rationalising situations more.

While you obviously won't be demonstrating this with your canine co-tutor in a way that puts them in a difficult situation, describing the zones and talking about the situations that are relevant to the dog can, as we discussed earlier, allow for a new level of empathy which, in turn, can lead to learning about human behaviour and turned into action.

This is where we use the *Approach and Retreat* technique, where people are encouraged to enter their stretch zones for short periods and then calmly retreat. This is a great model for use alongside goal setting, where people can target stretch zone activities to undertake for short periods. This may just be speaking in front of the group if it is a group you are running. It is also a lovely visual model that people can relate to easily.

Now you've thought about some of the ways in which you can use tried and tested theories while developing plenty of your own and adapting them all to benefit the people you will be working with, it's time to get down to business.

Chapter Two: Your Idea

Whether you think you can, or you think you can't. You're right.
Henry Ford

You have an idea, a genius idea, to work with dogs to help change the lives of humans for the better. You know that you're onto something, and you know that you can make a difference. Now, how do you turn all of that energy, passion and motivation into a sustainable business?

You start at the very beginning! Take time to formulate your idea, think through what it is you're actually going to offer and what your vision is for your CPPD business. Give yourself some time to focus on these early stages, as they will give you the foundations from which your future decisions can be based on.

In the excitement, there's also quite often a need for someone to play devil's advocate, to challenge the ideas and to offer a sounding board. That's what we're here for. It won't be long before you're so engrossed in your business that it might be difficult to take a step back and see the bigger picture. If you're going to be investing your time, money and energy into this venture, then you obviously want it to succeed. As the adage goes, 'people don't plan to fail, they fail to plan.'

Being in business is something that needs a serious amount of consideration. It's not for everybody, and yet there is no doubt that many people would be incredible in business if they took the leap. Being honest about what it involves, the pros and cons, and then taking the time to have an honest conversation with yourself about whether it's what you want, will start you off on the right track. There will be a wave of excitement as you know for sure that this is the path for you, a cold chill that runs through you as you know for sure it's not the path for you, or somewhere in between as you embark on this journey with trepidation and a knowing grin that all will be well.

From our experience, there's a mix of emotions, quite often on a daily basis, which is part of the adventure of running a social business. The highs and the lows come with equal intensity, and it is absolutely worth it.

You will be in charge. Your business, your rules! The direction in which you want to go is down to you, and all of the logistics can be chosen by you. Where you work, when you work and who you work with will all be your call. There's no limit to what you can achieve, how much social impact you can create, and the possibilities are, quite literally, endless. You can also change your mind, take your business in another direction, and that is ok too.

With all of those autonomous benefits comes the reality that you will probably find yourself working long hours, possibly without holidays, and there's nobody other than yourself to call and request a sick day. You will be faced with decisions you might not be equipped to make, and will have to quickly figure out what to do and how to do it. If things don't work out, there's nobody else to blame and that can take its toll on finances and self-confidence. *Sounds great, doesn't it?!*

When the going gets tough, which it will, being able to focus on why you decided to take this route and develop this business will help you through the difficult days and will be something to celebrate every day. Let's start at the beginning and get your ideas down on paper.

Congratulations, you're about to start your CPPD business.

What is your idea? *Describe it in a way that a 10-year-old would understand. No jargon and get everything out of your brain and onto paper.*

What sparked this idea?

What excites you about this idea?

Why does this idea have to become a social business?

What difference will this idea make?

What experience do you have that will help you to develop this idea? *Don't worry if there's a big space here, we're all learning all of the time and we'll help you to create a plan throughout this book.*

Have you tested this idea? *Have you started running sessions, spoken to potential partners or sought ideas... have you told anyone?*

Who will pay for this?

In order to take this idea and turn it into an articulate, focused and authentic business you need the foundations on which to build upon. These are especially important in social business, as you will need (and want) to be able to easily explain your social mission and measure your social impact against it.

This is the 'big picture' stuff. You wouldn't, we assume, find a piece of land and a few bricks and start building your dream home? You'd at least have a drawing of what you'd like it to look like in the end before placing the first brick? These elements will help you to design your dream.

At first, your vision, mission and values can feel quite similar. However, there are subtle differences that will force you to think about exactly what you want to achieve and how you are going to make this work.

Looking to the future, you can dream big (*we urge you to dream big!*) and state your aspirations with pride. That will be your *vision*. You will be able to clearly articulate exactly what you will achieve, for whom and how you will do it. That will be your *mission*. You will be transparent about your ethos and the culture of your business. These will be your *values*.

Vision

Start with the end in mind. Your vision is your ultimate destination, the reason you get out of bed in the morning, the inspiration to keep you going. This is one sentence that explains the change you are going to make in the world. Make it clear, concise and memorable. This will communicate exactly what you are going to achieve.

This is the time to state exactly how incredible your idea is, to dream big and allow yourself to aspire to become the leader in your field because you are about to change the world.

Mission

Without a mission statement, you risk wandering off course. This is easy to do, especially in the early days when any opportunity could be considered 'worth a try'. When resources are low and you're not progressing as quickly as you'd hoped, it is not unusual to find yourself saying 'yes' to all sorts of things that could be tenuously linked to your original idea. With a clear, thought through mission statement, you will have a guide to direct you towards the opportunities that will take your closer to your vision, and those that will not and are worth saying 'thank you, but no' to.

Make a list of the companies you respect and/or know well. Find their mission statements and see if they match your experience and understanding of the company. Reading those of other people can fuel your imagination; just be careful to stay true to your own ideas when writing your own mission. That way it is an authentic reflection of your business, and one you can trust in order to base your decisions on.

This statement is usually a short paragraph stating:

- Who your business is serving.

- What you provide.

- How you provide it.

- Why you are unique.

Remember that this is the vehicle that will take you to destination 'vision'.

Values

Values are intrinsically linked to social business and, as such, it can feel like a waste of time to state them. However, the details matter. Your values will help you to decide who you work with and who you don't. That is not necessarily linked to who you're working with directly, but who you choose to bank with, which designer you commission, who you advertise with, or who provides your equipment.

Don't be surprised if you are asked about these things, as you will be living your values, by virtue of the person you are and the business you have chosen to run. Be honest and state the values your business is proud to operate within. These will help when you are choosing the partners you work with, the outsourcing and the staff/volunteers you engage with. Saying you're passionate about dog welfare and then leaving your dog in the car for hours while you're running a session will speak louder than any words you have proclaimed. *We know you wouldn't do that, it's just an example!*

Now that you have taken the time to explore these ideas, you have the start of a business plan. A business plan doesn't have to be an epic document, unless that's how you work best, of course. A business plan needs to be a working document, something that you can benefit from and refer to. Having this starting point gives you a secure basis from which to make decisions about the practicalities of your business.

There's something that none of us want to think about, but that does have to be considered when making long-term plans. It's not unusual to be inspired by one particular dog when designing a business working with humans and canines. It's not unusual that the lessons learned by one particular dog transcend the immediate family, and they become a catalyst for change for many more people. It's not unusual for businesses, projects, programmes and charities to be inspired by one particular dog.

What happens when that dog is no longer with us? There's a familiar quote that says the only real failing of a dog is that they don't live for long enough. For anyone who has experienced loss, no truer words have ever been spoken.

The harsh reality is that a business has to be considered in a sustainable way. If a business is centred around the skills, character or presence of one dog, there will be exceptionally difficult times ahead.

Going back to work without the inspiration behind the business is difficult to comprehend. If that dog was central to business activities, it is impossible. This is not something to ignore, but something to acknowledge and plan for as part of your business strategy.

There will be much more about the dogs later on the book, as they are the fundamental part of a CPPD business, but this is something that we have both been forced to consider; and while we know it's tempting to bury our heads deep into the nearest sandpit, the harsh reality of life without our inspiration and best friend has to be faced.

That's enough doom and gloom for now though. Onwards and upwards as we talk about you. After all, without you, the dog won't have a job to go to!

Chapter Three: You First

Believe in yourself. You are braver than you think,
more talented than you know,
and capable of more than you imagine.
Roy T. Bennett

What's your story? In this section of the book it's all about you. You can have a dog with you, you can absolutely have a dog or multiple dogs who are part of your story, but this is all about YOU.

It has to be all about you, as you are the person who is going to drive your idea and turn it into a reality.

What does it take to run a social business? There's a difference between personality traits and skill sets when it comes to running a business. However, both can be developed, learnt, and if necessary, outsourced. Yes, personality traits can be outsourced! For example, if you don't like talking to people on the phone, there are amazing people out there who'll do that for you, just like an accountant can file your tax return or a designer can create your logo.

To begin with, rest assured that you don't have to turn into a different person in order to run a successful business. On the contrary, it's who you are that will make this business a success.

There's a little secret we'd like to share with you before we go any further. It's going to rock your world and change everything you thought you knew about running a business. Are you ready?

Here it is...

Even though this is your dream, most of the time you're not going to feel like doing the things you know you have to do!

Do you think we wanted to write this book? *Absolutely, Yes.* Do you think we talked about it a lot? *Absolutely, Yes.* Do you think we leapt straight to the laptops and excitedly tapped at the keys? *Absolutely, Not!* There was procrastination, more talking, more procrastination, and lots of tea before we actually typed the first words, which have since been deleted and rewritten numerous times.

You see, that doesn't change when you run your own business. Living the dream, in reality, is only a process of executing your ideas. You can have all the ideas in the world, they could be the most amazing ideas that have ever graced the planet, but unless you take action, that's all they'll ever be.

We have been asked by hundreds of people for help and advice about starting a CPPD business. Some of the ideas we've been told about are mind-blowing. Pure genius has come spilling out the mouths of enthusiastic people with life-changing ideas based on their experiences, their stories and their expertise. How many of those people have subsequently taken action and brought those ideas to life? Not many. It's all in the execution!

So, back to you!

Write down five things you like about yourself. Go on, we dare you! Just do it; nobody is going to read this unless you would like them to. Five things... GO.

1.

2.

3.

4.

5.

You're going to have to get used to selling your ideas, and those ideas have come from YOU. The five things you wrote down are going to be five of the (many) reasons people will want to work with you.

If you didn't write down five things, go back and do it now. What will motivate you to do it? Whatever it is that motivates you, keep that in mind for the future, as along this journey to creating the business of your dreams you're going to have to do a lot of things you don't want to do. There'll be things that make you uncomfortable, and things that your inner dialogue is fighting. In this case, tell that little voice to 'shush' and be honest about five things you like about who you are.

That's a little insight into what it feels like to run your own business. It can be uncomfortable, it can make you vulnerable, it will bring your thoughts into written and spoken form; they will be real. It feels good too though, right?!

Resilience is one of the key elements that you'll need to develop to get started, and to keep going throughout the ongoing business journey you're starting. That is a skill that can absolutely be learnt, and one that our dogs are incredible teachers of. You have brought your dog into the home of another species, and other than the occasional miscommunication about whether the carpet should be used for toilet purposes, we guess you're all doing ok at sharing a home? You gradually introduced your dog to the human world, to the rules and regulations that frankly make very little sense, and built their resilience until they rock living with their human family and all the nuances that involves.

That's what you need to do for yourself now. You're entering a new, and possibly alien, world of CPPD business. Rocking your CPPD business isn't a destination, it's a lifestyle choice. It's going to mean continual learning and edging further out of your comfort zone day by day, until it's second nature. Along the way, you'll find things that simply don't suit you at all. With your dog, you encourage and nurture the elements of their character and natural skill set that enable them to succeed. In the case of you and your CPPD business, you won't be able to do it all, so nurture the areas you know you can rock, and look at outsourcing, or bringing in a team to support you in the other areas.

What do you think it takes to run a successful CPPD business?

What personality traits do you have that will help your CPPD business to succeed?

What skills do you have that will help your CPPD business to succeed?

What else will you need to help your CPPD business to succeed?

Who else will you need to help your CPPD business to succeed? *This doesn't have to be a named person, as you might not know this person yet, but you do need to know who you're looking for so you'll know when you've found them!*

We don't know what it is going to take for YOU to run YOUR successful business. That depends on who you are, what skills you bring, and what you'll need to develop. It also depends on the business you want to run. This isn't a rule book, there isn't a 'right' way of doing this. We are different people, running different business in different ways; we just have a common theme, enjoy working together and enjoy a similar level of procrastination. Great teams have been built on much less! Relax and do this YOUR WAY.

As the self-doubt creeps in, go back to your vision and remember why you started.

One way you can explore the areas you excel at, and those areas you might need support with, are through personality tests. Links to some of our favourites can be found on our website. These offer a wonderful insight, and there are so many available that you'll be able to find one that resonates with you. One of the many benefits of these tests is to enable you to determine what else you might need to run your business. Please note, the word is 'need', not 'want'. If you are an action orientated person who is permanently operating at 100 miles per hour, you might need someone around you who is more reflective. That person might not be someone you would choose to work with, because you like decisions to be made quickly and to take action yesterday, but they could be exactly what you need. Or, they could hold you up and drive you to distraction. Unless you have thought this through, you could make a decision that leads to tension, unhappiness and potentially the end of your business. Likewise, if you are somebody who needs structure, a clear plan and a daily update of how the actions are being met, working with someone who goes with the flow, could be the best, or worst, decision of your life. There isn't a right or wrong, we're simply urging you to consider what you need in order to make your CPPD business a success.

You can also think about your ideal day and learn about what motivates you, then build your business around this notion.

What does your ideal working day look like? If this is going to be your new way of life, then it's worth thinking about what you want it to look like in a practical sense, not just in an abstract way through your vision.

Describe your ideal working day.

Will you be around people or working on your own?

Will you be in a specific work-related premises or at home?

What time of day do you work best... and does this fit the lifestyle you wish to live?

How much travelling are you happy to do?

Where will you base yourself for the 'business tasks' – admin, letters, planning etc?

Is the location conducive to successfully completing these tasks? *One of us does a lot of work online and moved to a remote part of the Welsh countryside where broadband is yet to be discovered. We're just saying 'think it through'!*

How will this impact on the dog(s) who are part of your business, and how do you feel about that?

To make your CPPD business a success, these elements all need to come together to support you to work in a way that brings out the best in you and resonates with the ethos of work you're doing.

When people set goals, and the success of your business will potentially be one of the biggest goals you set, there is a common theme around why things don't work out. The theme is that the goal and the lifestyle needed to reach that goal aren't in congruence:

- If part of the business aim is to be able to spend more time with your family, who are in school or in 9-5 jobs, you need to ensure your target audience don't only need your services during evenings and weekends.

- If you love the idea of spending more time at home with your dog, make sure that you can happily work alone, that you can structure your day, and that you don't need people around you to bounce ideas off and engage with.

- If you need to have people around you, is there a business hub near you? Is it dog-friendly?

We urge you to consider all of the elements that will make up your business before you get started. Not to put you off - on the contrary; to enable you to succeed at a faster rate. Taking the time to think these things through now will help you to create your dream business in a practical sense, as well as ensuring you can work towards your vision without compromising your own health and wellbeing.

On that note, your health and wellbeing have to be your top priority. Yes, your TOP priority. You are your business now. If you're not in tip top condition, how are you going to make this work and how will you have the emotional and physical resources to help and support the people you're working with? You are an ambassador for your business, and going into a CPPD business there will usually be an element of wellbeing in the widest sense, forming part of your message. Are you a true ambassador for your message? *We'll leave that thought with you!*

We have talked briefly about the dog(s) being part of the message, and that there could be a specific dog who has been the catalyst for your work, along with an experience or story of your own. If your story is the catalyst, it's worth taking some time to consider what that means in the context of your business. Thinking ahead, you will probably be interviewed about the motivation behind your business, it will form part of the context when you speak at events or write articles to promote your work. It won't just be the people you're working with who are reading these articles and listening to you on the TV or radio. It will also be your family, your friends, your former work colleagues and your neighbour; you know, the one you drive past playing with your sat nav in order to avoid making eye contact?!

As part of your planning, take the time to write your story in a way that you are happy to share publicly. Share as much or as little as you are comfortable with. You can always share more at a later date, but you won't be able to delete anything from the public realm. You never have to share more than you are comfortable with. Your authenticity and integrity comes from who you are, not details you may or may not choose to share.

Your story needs to resonate with the people you're working with in a way that they will understand. It will use language that they identify with, it will acknowledge their fears, the obstacles that stand in their way, the fact you understand their story, and how your CPPD business will take them to a new chapter. How you do that is totally up to you.

Imagine that you are being interviewed by a journalist, where, for the record, nothing is 'off the record' (!) and you are caught off guard with their questions. They will probe and they will be direct. Even the kindest, most empathetic journalist needs to be able to share a story, not an idea. It's their job! You need to be ready. Growing your business will mean engaging with different forms of marketing, and being able to have maximum social impact means sharing your message far and wide so people know that you exist.

Decide on the narrative that you are happy to share, practice talking about it, practice sharing it and practice saying it with pride. It is often easier to share the narrative in front of total strangers, so be brave and ask your nearest and dearest to be your audience when you're ready. They'd probably rather hear it from you, in the comfort of your living room, than while driving to work listening to you being interviewed.

If you have stuck with this chapter, thought about the exercises and written down those thoughts. You are more than ready to get this show on the road. If you haven't, that's ok too! Think about what's coming up for you?

What has stopped you from taking the steps?

What do you need to do to remove the block?

Who do you need to talk with to help you at this stage?

When will you talk to that person or take the next step to move forward?

There are lots of ways that you can turn your idea into action. If you have reached this point of the book, and you're not sure you're at the start of a journey you wish to continue, but you know you want to do 'something', that's brilliant! Learning at this stage is much better than six months down the line when you're going to have a much harder time changing your ideas.

You can change your ideas; the vision might be exactly the same but the vehicle that takes you there (your mission) might need to be adapted or completely changed.

This is about YOU. It's your time, energy and investment that's going to make this happen, so getting these foundations right for you is worth the effort.

Chapter Four: Making Your CPPD Business a Reality

Petting, scratching, and cuddling a dog could be as soothing to the mind and heart as deep meditation and almost as good for the soul as prayer.
Dean Koontz

The thought of business planning is often enough to switch off even the most enthusiastic among us. You can take a risk, live life on the edge and follow your gut without a plan. Or, you can spend some time figuring out how this is going to work in reality. Give yourself some time to think through your ideas in a logical way, and plan the order in which you need to work to ensure you know what to do, and when you need to do it.

One tip we can offer from experience is to do all of the thinking before you start worrying about the legal structure of your business. The most important thing is that you have a business that works for you. It needs to be planned in such a way that you know who your audience will be, what you will be offering them, and how you will offer them what they need. If you have your heart set on a particular business structure, you might find you're adapting your business ideas to fit a model that won't serve you or the people you would like to work with. There will be a structure that fits your ideas and, if you're clear about what your business will offer, decisions about the structure come easily.

The plan can be in whatever format you want it to be. You might need to formalise it if you're approaching a bank, corporate sponsors, or tendering for work, but for now, make it something you'll enjoy working on. What do we say about working with dogs? It's all in the motivation! Start the way you mean to go on and take a lesson from our canine friends, motivate yourself to make this as enjoyable as possible, and you'll be pleasantly surprised by how the ideas flow.

Spreadsheets, huge pieces of paper, coloured pens, online planning apps, or a brand new shiny notebook; whatever you need to make this happen.

Picking up this book, we assume, means you already know how fabulous dogs are, how we can learn an incredible amount from them, and that in your particular area of expertise they have a profound effect on the humans you're working with. There's no doubt that your desire to work in this area will make a difference. Your business plan starts at this point, with all of the knowledge, experience and expertise you bring to your idea. It will act as a map to help you get to where you want to be, it will be a working document, and if you fancy veering off course at any point, it will help you to make decisions around whether that's an adventure worth trying or a risk that takes you too far off course.

Earlier in the book you considered your vision, mission and values. At least, we hope you did. If you skipped through that section, now's the time to revisit it. Remember that it's all about motivation and having an emotional connection, being able to articulate the passion you have for working with dogs in the way you do, and sharing that message in ways that will enable the people you're working with to stop and take notice is vital.

If you did the exercises earlier on, we're impressed and hope you'll 'click and treat' yourself before starting on this section!

We're going to go through a series of business planning questions and at the heart of each one needs to be the dog(s) you plan to work with. We'll be talking about some of the nuances of working with dogs in different settings later in the book, so for now, please keep in mind how you plan to operate and how the dog(s) will be nurtured through that process.

If your business involves travelling, how will that impact on the dog(s)? If your business involves working with groups or 121, how will that impact on the dog(s)? If you are planning to run consecutive sessions in a short period of time, how will that impact on the dog(s)? We know that the dog(s) are central to what you're doing, so they need to be central to the planning phase too, even if they're not hugely helpful at this stage!

These questions are designed to get you started in taking your idea forward. There will be lots of other areas you'll need to consider that are specific to your area of work. We would simply like to encourage you to think through whether your idea can be turned into a sustainable business and, in working through the questions, whether you think it's something you would like to pursue.

What is your business actually going to do? It sounds like a simple question, but give it some thought. Are you going to be running workshops? Who are you going to be working with? Are your participants coming to you or are you going to them? Are you working with people on a 121 basis or in groups? Are you working with your own dog(s)? Are you working with participants and their dog(s)? Are you going to be doing the work or do you have a team? There will be lots more questions as we go through this section, but write as much as you can in response to the question;

What is your business going to do?

How will this impact on the dog(s)?

What products and/or services are you going to provide to the people you will be working with? If you've decided that you're going to be running workshops, for example, what content will you be providing in those sessions? What will the learning objectives be? What theory of change will you be adopting to support your participants? Think about all of the different ways you could reach people and from there, you might come up with new ideas for products and/or services that you can offer.

What products and/or services are you going to provide?

How will this impact on the dog(s)?

How will the people you're working with access these fabulous products and services that you are providing? There could be different answers if you have a range of ideas, so think through each one. Are people buying online, are they travelling to your facility, are you going to them? Are you all meeting in a huge training field and embracing the outdoors? If so, are there toilets for the humans and somewhere to make a cuppa?!

How will the people you're working with access your products and services?

How will this impact on the dog(s)?

The dreaded word; pricing! Money has to play a part in order for your business to become sustainable. Now's the time to think about how you would like to be paid for the work you are doing. Will you be looking for funding? Will you be charging for your products and services? If so, who will be paying? Will it be the participants themselves, or the services the access who commission your work? Will you be looking for sponsorship? Do different products and services have different options within your pricing structure? Will one element of the business pay for another element? We'll be talking more about this within social enterprise models, but for now, be creative.

Alongside the monetary fun, you'll need to pay for marketing, insurance, venues, travel, sausages... the list of outgoings is extensive and will depend on what you're offering. This has to play a part in the pricing plan so you know that all expenses are considered.

There can be barriers that come up when we start thinking about money. For many of us, working with dogs and with people who resonate with us, involves a personal story that has been the catalyst to the idea. A personal mission is vital when we are developing our work, but that does not mean that the work we're doing shouldn't be paid for. We pay our dogs for a job well done. We pay them handsomely when we want a behaviour to be repeated with enthusiasm, and we value the process. We deserve to embrace that same process. You deserve to be paid for a job well done. Now's your chance to think about how that will happen and how to ensure it's in monetary form, not sausages.

Who will pay for each product and service I offer?

What will the price(s) be for each product and service I offer?

How will this impact on the dog(s)? *You might think that this side of the planning isn't about the dog(s), but remember that they're working, too. For example, if you need to double the amount of sessions you're delivering to make the numbers add up, then there's a direct impact on the dog(s).*

Who are you going to be working with? Whoever they are, let's hope they like dogs! The more you know about the people you would like to work with, the more likely you are to design the perfect products and services for them.

If your business has stemmed from a personal experience, that doesn't necessarily mean that you have the additional knowledge and expertise necessary to deliver professional services. Likewise, if you have a professional background in this field, do you have the personal touch that will be needed to bring this idea to life? There's no right or wrong answer to this, and only you know what awesome skills you have already and what you might need to develop in order to make this a life changing offering to the people you want to work with. We're all a work in progress and we're all continually learning. Knowing where to focus our skill development in the limited time we have can begin with answering these questions, as we can find out where the gaps are, which can only be a good thing.

Think about the person you would most like to work with. *Get to know them better than you know your dog!* Think through everything about them, as you need to be talking to this person as you develop your products and services. This is the person you will be marketing to, and this is the person whose life you are going to change.

Describe this person.

How will this person impact on the dog(s)?

Do you have a name for your business? Write down your ideas and think about whether the name(s) you like will resonate with the person you have just described. When you have your shortlist, you'll need to find out if that name already exists with another business, if it is available for you to use, and you can then start thinking about logo design, websites, marketing and all of the fun and games that go with turning your idea into a tangible business. You thought through all of this in your pricing plans, though didn't you? *Didn't you...?!*

What will my business be called?

How will this impact on the dog(s)? *Again, this might sound like a silly question, but think it through! If there is one dog who features in your business name or logo, what happens when that dog is not able to be a part of the business. Will that affect the way you market your products and services and how will it affect you? It's not something we want to think about in the excitement of a new venture, but building a sustainable business means planning for the long-term.*

Will you be working by yourself, or are you going into business with someone else? Will you build a team of employees or are you hoping to work with volunteers? How will this be managed? If you are planning to expand your team, you'll need to familiarise yourself with employment law and be clear about how the team will benefit the business and help you to achieve your goals.

If you do decide to work by yourself, it's unrealistic to think you can do everything that running a business requires. Think about who you will potentially be outsourcing some of the work to; freelancers working on your logo design, or a website developer, an accountant or bookkeeper? Who will you need to help you utilise your time in the best possible way?

Who will be working with me?

How will this impact on the dog(s)?

Is there anyone else doing this work? Check out the competition. Find out what they're doing and how they're doing it. Learn from them.

Think about the person you described earlier. Why will they choose to work with you and not your competitor?

How will this impact on the dog(s)? *Ok, this one might not affect the dog(s)!*

Is there a social need for your business? This is an interesting question because arguably, if you have conceived this idea, benefitted or seen other people benefit from working with dogs in the way you're proposing, then 'yes', there is a need. Working in an innovative and creative way might mean that there isn't a precedent for your work, yet you categorically know that, given the chance, you can make a difference.

So, let's cut to the chase. Will people pay you for your products and services?

How will you go about testing this and finding out if the people you would like to work with (or the services they access) will pay for your products and services?

How will this impact on the dog(s)?

As you start to discuss the business idea and research the social need, you will also need to consider how you are going to measure the impact you are having. This is important whether you are applying for funding or asking people to pay for your products and services, as you will have to prove that working with dogs in this way is beneficial. Even though we *know* it's beneficial, we still have to evidence it.

From now, think about how you will measure the progress of the participants you are working with. What is it you would like to change about their behaviour? What is it you would like them to experience? What changes will they make to their lives as a result of working with you?

What social impact will you measure and how will you measure it?

How will this impact on the dog(s)?

What else will you need to make this happen? Use this space to free your mind of the ideas that have come to you as you have been answering the questions. There are some questions to prompt you, and we urge you to write down anything that will help you to take your idea forward. Use this space to also write down actions you need to take. For example, if you don't know what insurance you'll need or how much it will cost, make an action to investigate this. Researching now will help to reduce surprises in the future!

Now that you have everything you need to take your idea forward, it's time to start thinking about the legal structure in which you would like to work. As you have chosen to pick up this book, and you're choosing to use your passion for working with dogs to make the world a better place, we are assuming that there is a social mission attached to your business.

You might have heard the term 'social enterprise' in relation to the sort of work you're starting. A 'social enterprise' isn't determined by the legal structure, only by the work that is undertaken. You can choose to work as a sole trader with a social mission and be regarded as a social enterprise.

There are numerous legal structures available, and each one will have an impact on how you can access funding, the governance requirements and your personal liability. Having a clear idea about how you want your business to operate will mean you can now look at the options and explore the best way forward for you and your business.

When you're buzzing about your idea, getting excited about how you can, and will, make an incredible difference in the world, this part of the process can be a bit of a fun-snatcher. However, if you really want to take your concept out into the world and grab the attention of the people who need your help, you have to be ready.

A legal structure will clarify the responsibilities you have as a business owner. This has a direct impact on the way you are viewed by funders, investors and partners. With a structure comes accountability and, in turn, evidence about how you operate. There are rules about the paperwork you need to complete, the taxes you will need to pay, and how you can personally profit from the business.

If you have been through the questions and feel that your idea doesn't lend itself to a business, then you have other options, such as an 'unincorporated association' where you can run a voluntary club or group and not make a profit. Whatever idea you have, there is a way to develop it.

In the United Kingdom, the most popular legal structures for social enterprise are;

- Community Interest Company (this can be limited by shares or by guarantee)
- Industrial & Provident Society (this is a type of mutual society)
- Company Limited by Shares
- Company Limited by Guarantee

There is also the charity model, which could be something for you to consider, depending on the answers to the questions throughout the book so far.

We have a number of links at our website, along with case studies, interviews and words of wisdom from people working with dogs to create social change.

Congratulations on making it to the end of this section. As a reward, we are now going to talk about dogs!

Chapter Five: Partnership Working With Dogs; the reality, the fun and the heartache!

A dog is so often the answer.
When you're lonely and need company,
or when you're tired of company and need lonely.
Robert Brault

Presumably if you have got this far you are really serious about working alongside dogs, with all the benefits they can provide. You have already thought now about your business structure, your CPPD vision, and many of the practicalities you will need to make this happen.

Now let's talk about the dogs. 'About time', we hear you say!

We, of course, totally get the desire to partner with dogs to provide awesome interventions. As you know, we are familiar with people saying to us 'I'd love to do what you do, my dog would be so good at it because…'. This chapter looks at the reality of that dream and aims to cover many of the questions we wish we had asked ourselves right at the beginning of our enterprises, as well as some ideas to get you started working in partnership with your dog or other canine co-tutors.

Start by asking yourself some preliminary questions.

Do you intend to work with your own dog/s?

Yes or No

You've probably guessed that whether you answered yes or no, there are some more questions for you! Here goes:

Do you actually have a dog you feel is suitable yet? Or are you intending to get one at some point in the future?

How do you/will you know that your dog is suitable?

If your dog is ill or out of action, what can you offer in your sessions?

Do you have a back-up plan for if your dog does not enjoy what you're planning to do? As we well know, you can never assume anything where dogs are concerned.

What criteria are you using to make sure the dog/s you work with are suitable?

Are the dogs you are using relevant to your project aims and objectives and/or your target group?

How many sessions do you intend to do with each dog per week?
How will you assess your dog's tiredness and their capability to
work?

How far will you travel to a session?

Does your dog like travelling in the car?

What will you do it the weather is very hot... or more likely in the UK, very cold?

Are you appropriately qualified and/or experienced to assess the dogs emotional and physical wellbeing, as well as to interpret body language cues and information, all while running a people focussed session.

What level of training does your dog need for your project activities; do they have it? How will you maintain it during the programme/s? What will you do if they don't have it?

If you do not intend to partner with your own dogs, then whose will you be working alongside?

Do you have a link with a rescue organisation? We will explore that aspect further on.

Are you going to 'borrow' a dog? If so, how well do you know that dog? Do you know how that dog behaves in a way you require when they're not with his/her usual guardian? Dogs can be very different when they're not with their guardian.

Are there any insurance considerations for working with other people's dogs in this context?

If you intend to use dogs currently in the care of a rescue organisation, whose insurance covers that?

What else has come to mind in relation to your specific project(s) while you've been thinking about these questions? Write it all down before you forget!

Now let's address some of these issues in more detail.

Partnership: Working with your own dog(s).

This is usually people's preferred option. After all, it is great to share your dogs with others and see the benefits they can bring. The thought of getting paid for spending time with your dog is very attractive. However, building your business around one dog (especially an 'untested' dog) is a risky enterprise and has limitations. If this is your plan, then you need to pay special attention to really knowing your dog. Obviously, you need to take into consideration your dog's age, temperament, abilities, strengths and any potential difficulties. Most therapy and visiting organisations do not recommend working with a dog under 1 year, nor one that you have lived with for less than 6 months. However, these guidelines are basic and only the very beginning of what you will need to think about.

The intensity of your planned workload.

How many and what type of sessions do you intend your dog to do each week? Depending on the nature of your sessions and your programme, the work can be very tiring for the dogs. Remember the dogs are working as partners- their behaviour will be giving you cues for discussion- they are not passive in the process.

The nature of your sessions.

How do you actually intend to involve your dog? Will your project sessions be lively and interactive? Will you be including hands on activities for people with your dog/s? How much of this is it appropriate for your dog to do? There are no guidelines here, as each dog and each project will be completely different. It will be a continuing process of assessing and monitoring your dog for signs of stress or tiredness, or sometimes just disinterest! Are you intending that your dog is more likely to be a calming influence in the room, there for people to stroke and love, and as a welcome distraction, without any specific requirements? In which case, what happens if they want to get up and join in? Or if they, in true dog fashion, decide they want to be more involved and stop you delivering the session you're being paid to deliver?

These considerations will affect what your dog's role can be. From our experience, most dogs will have something to offer in the right environment. Regardless of the nature of your project they will need to be happily controllable, enjoy the company of different people, welcome and encourage engagement, and not be too insecure or clingy to their handler/owner. It's pretty handy if you can have a conversation without them feeling the need to join in!

Your dog and stress.

It is likely that your dog may experience some stress, as will you. This may be initial stress at entering new environments, occasional stress related to particular clients, stress at being handled differently to how they are accustomed, or receiving different cues for behaviours. There will potentially be unexpected and unpredictable stress (for example, it is not easy to discover how your dog would cope if you were in a school when the fire alarm goes off and you are both leaving the building with 1200 students... until it happens... which it did!)

How much stress do you think it is appropriate for your dog to handle? Some may say 'none'. Realistically we see stress as a necessary part of learning and growing. You might get stressed in a session yourself. It is likely that project participants will be stressed at some point, either just by getting there, by external life situations, by being part of the group, or by being expected to talk in public. Experiencing some level of stress, within healthy limits of time and intensity, is part of life for all creatures. As a rule, toxic chemicals released during stressful situations can be reabsorbed by the body with no negative long term effects. It is when stress becomes a fairly constant state with no periods of relaxation and ease that the effects become negative. People and dogs in this situation can become hyper vigilant, and continually increase their own stress levels by heightened responses to stressors/triggers.

You need to be clear about your stance and understanding of stress, both for you and your dog. Some dogs, like some people, are naturally more resilient and better able to cope with stress than others. Exposure to stress in a controlled way can build this resilience, which might be a good model for your client group as well as building resilience in your dog. All at the same time. That's a pretty cool thing right there!

You need to be clear about your stance on stress. It may well be different to ours, and that's ok!

What are your thoughts about the implications of stress for you and any dog you hope to work alongside in relation to your CPPD business? How will you manage this?

Dogs, change and health.

Dogs change. What your dog enjoys now, they may not enjoy later as they enter a different life stage. What will be your back up plan for changing the focus of your activities if needed?

Dogs get ill and injured. What if your dog gets injured or sick? What about if your dog gets injured at a session? What if they're out of action recuperating for weeks? What's your back up plan?

Dogs get old. They can get creaky, sore and less energetic. Pain can make dogs (and people!) grumpy and sensitive. This can change what they can tolerate and how much they like being handled. How will you know when the time is right to retire your dog from some, or all, of your activities? We have read articles of hospital visiting dogs being wheeled along in prams/trolleys who can no longer walk. How do you feel about this?

Dogs die. Tough, but true. Obviously, you will need to manage your own personal grief about losing your partner. In addition, you will have to manage your grief as far the project is concerned. You may need to help others with their loss as well, if your dog is well known to project participants. Are you up to this? How can you tell if you are up to this, before it happens? Will you be able to discuss this openly with clients and present the information in an appropriate way? If you use images of your dog in your work what does this mean for your promotional material?

Dogs and dog training

As we know, there are many different opinions about dog training. We would advise you to explore them all so you know what's going on and what you could be up against, but obviously to use force free, kind dog training methods based on scientific evidence and research. This isn't just the only option for a positive relationship with your canine co-tutor, but will be a great resource for discussion and role modelling for your client group. Depending on the nature of your project, be prepared for people to not agree with what you believe in and the way to interact with your dog.

How well trained does your dog have to be? This really depends on what you are actually asking of him or her. For some projects a high level of training may be essential, for others the dog's natural behaviour may be the learning tool. The experience of working with highly trained agility dogs - you know, the kind that almost do it by themselves - could be great fun and provides a feel-good factor for participants, but it would not necessarily teach them a whole lot. Working with dogs who can 'do' agility if the team's communication skills are good enough is a better vehicle for discussing communication skills, learning cycles, and motivation in many respects. There's also the added benefit of people feeling fabulous when it works! Working with rescue dogs with basic training is empowering for participants, as the dogs can make huge changes in short periods of time. Working with a very lively dog can be good for working with those with ADHD, but then so can working with a calm dog. You need to know what you want to work on with the people you're working with in order to ensure you have the right canine co-tutor by your side.

Take some time to think about what you need, and if you really have it. If you don't have it, what do you have? How can this be useful for your work?

One word of caution: you will need to be prepared for people to handle your dog(s) in ways you may not like, or that are different to how you would want your canine co-tutor to be handled. How will you deal with this and maintain the safe environment you need to enable learning and personal development?

If you have a dog trained to a level you're happy with, it might be that exposure to different groups of people will confuse your dog and result in some of your training getting (temporarily) 'lost'. How will you feel if that happens?

If you train using treats, and your client group are not able to reward at the time/intensity your dog is accustomed to, will your dog get frustrated, and how will you deal with this?

Working with rescue dogs.

If your plan is to work with rescue dogs, this is an incredible learning tool and metaphor for many of the things you may wish to cover in your sessions. This is especially true if your target group includes children in care or adopted children, abuse survivors, anyone who has felt abandoned, or people who have experienced trauma. With any group, rescue dogs are great for developing empathy and resilience, as well as learning about responsible dog ownership and welfare.

However, for many rescue organisations it is just not possible to allow you to use their dogs. There are so many considerations for them. These include insurance implications, the location of your sessions, taking the dog off-site, kennel opening times, while the dog is out with you they will not be visible and therefore could miss an adoption opportunity, and there could be concerns about their behaviour. Dogs who are living in rescue kennels do not always display their best behaviour.

Will the dog(s) be able to cope? Careful assessment needs to be undertaken before using dogs from a rescue centre, in partnership with that centre. Will a member of staff from the rescue be accompanying the dog? If not, how much time will you be putting in to get to know the dog before using him or her for your sessions?

If a dog is in a foster home, more may be known about the dog's behaviour and temperament. Will the foster carers be happy to come and handle the dog while you are using him/her? If the foster carer is there, will it impact on the dog's ability to interact with the group? How much time do you have to get to know the dog prior to doing any work with him/her.

We often get asked, 'how do you actually BEGIN to get started with your dog?' If you have an untried, untested dog that you are keen to use in your professional practice, it can be quite daunting to work out how to actually get going and find that start point. Not all dogs like doing all things.

One way is for you and your dog to volunteer for one of the charities who use visiting dogs. The best of them will:

- Independently assess your dog out in the real world
- Provide training, guidelines and resources
- Provide branded clothes
- Provide places to visit, or help you find our own
- Provide ongoing support
- Pay mileage

There are links to some of these charities on our website. Don't be put off if their headquarters are miles away from you; most offer a nationwide service. Do your research, as always some will be more organised and effective than others. One might be a better 'fit' for you and what you eventually hope to achieve. If you take this route,

you'll be volunteering your time, but what you do and when/where
you do it is ultimately up to you and it can be a great way to get
going before investing in a new business. Also, from a business
perspective it doesn't do any harm to say your dog has been
assessed and is suitable to work for a national charity.

With all that in mind, here are some more questions for you to
think about. Don't worry if you can't answer them all yet, they are
still worth considering.

After reading this, have you had any new ideas about the dog(s) you
are planning to use?

Make a list of your dog's strengths and why you think he/she she
will be good at this type of work.

Now make a list of those things you think your dog may find challenging.

What can you be doing now to improve that situation.

What challenges do you foresee with your dog related plans?

Do you feel you need to learn more about dog behaviour/body language/signs of stress in dogs?

Can you explore these avenues while setting up your business, or are there things you need to do first?

So, now we have the dog stuff sorted, it's back to business.

Chapter Six: What Do You Do Next?

When you're curious, you find lots of interesting things to do. And one thing it takes to accomplish something is courage.

Walt Disney

You have done well to get to this stage. The ground work is complete, and now you know which direction your business is taking. We hope that this is an exciting feeling for you, a combination of fear, intrigue and exhilaration? We know from our dogs that curiosity leads to incredible adventures and occasionally a roll in some sh*t, so we encourage you to be curious as you start putting your ideas into action, see where it takes you, and don't let the inevitable roll in sh*t every so often put you off. Just shake it off and move on!

One of the common questions we get asked is 'So what do you actually do?' That's a fine question. It's one that you're going to need to be able to answer in a succinct and practical way, and it will hopefully be closely aligned to your mission. If it isn't, it's time to go back to the start of the book! What will you actually do?

The idea isn't enough anymore. Now, it's all about the details. When you explore the learning theory that suits your idea, and the way in which you can make tangible changes with the humans and dogs you're connecting with, you must be able to evidence what you're doing and how you can make an impact. You'll potentially be talking with established organisations: charities, schools, health and social care providers, or rehabilitation services. These organisations will need a professional submission that details what you will be doing, how you will be doing it, and what you aim to achieve by doing it. You might also be approaching funders who will need to see exactly where their money is going and how it will be used to make sustainable change. This is when the research, the late nights, and the copious amounts of tea (or coffee, whatever you need!) come into play.

There are hundreds of ways that you can start to create your business with the foundations you have begun working on throughout this book. What we're going to do now is take you through some headline stages and it's totally up to you to decide whether you need them, how you can adapt them to suit your business, and how you can follow the process in a way that makes sense to you. There's no right and wrong, it's just that sometimes when we're starting out, we don't know what we don't know and therefore don't always know what to ask. One thing we do get asked is 'how' we started our businesses. Needless to say, we did things differently! However, we asked ourselves questions based on the stages below and decided what would be the best way forward at each stage.

On our website, we have a series of links to guidance notes, frameworks, business planning methods and links to the businesses who feature in our case studies, so that you can see what other people are doing and how they're doing it. The case studies are coming up next, but they're not going to tell you what you need to do. You're the only person who can do that, and you're the best person to do that.

An Advisory Group

Call it whatever you like; an advisory group, a steering group, a board; whatever you call it, and whatever form it takes as part of your structure, get yourself some people to talk with. You will need people who can help you to see the bigger picture, people who have specific expertise and can answer questions in a way that's relevant to your business, people who can help you make tough decisions, and people you can celebrate with when your plans have come to life and you're changing lives. We're not saying that you have to have meetings for the sake of meetings, or bring everyone together in a conference room for a death-by-Powerpoint session; after all, that's why we're embracing self-employment, right? You can manage this group in a way that works for you; just please get some support. This group might vary depending on the projects you're working on, and you might have different people involved in different elements of the business. That's great and vital to move each stage forward. That's also why it's even more important to have a group, as defined by you, who can help you to keep a strategic focus, remind you about your vision and mission, and support you in growing your business in a way that serves you.

Depending on the legal structure you choose, you might have specific requirements for this group and, as such, seek out people who have specific expertise. You will need to ensure that these people also support your values, understand the business vision, and understand their role within the structure. Having clearly defined roles and responsibilities will help to keep people on track, and if you're asking people to volunteer their time, being able to state exactly what the role will involve will manage expectations and ensure you get the right person who can willingly dedicate the time you need.

Decide upon your role within the group. That might sound silly. However, this is your idea that's coming to life, and something that you no doubt have a personal affinity with. Therefore, there's a teeny tiny chance that objectivity might be lacking on occasion. To make the most of the group and to allow them to challenge you, offer constructive criticism and help you to grow, you might want to consider bringing in someone to facilitate discussions and / or take notes.

Market Research

We know that you have an amazing idea and that you are passionate about making a change. There could be lots of different ways to execute that idea, and that's where market research comes in. Have you explored the market you're about to enter, your competitors and your target audience? The market and your competitors aren't necessarily other CPPD businesses. It's more likely that they're other service providers seeking to support the clients you would like to work with. For example, there are numerous opportunities within the area of youth justice, and working to prevent young people from reoffending. Why would an organisation commission you and your canine team as opposed to the other four social enterprises who have approached them from a fitness perspective, an arts perspective, or a business development perspective. Obviously, you have a dog and you're the best one, we know this, we just want you to be able to convince them!

You can sit at your computer and find out everything you can about your competition, or if it's appropriate for what you're offering, your potential partners. Sometimes, a joint submission with shared objectives can be a great opportunity, and it's through research that you'll find out the options.

You can head out to talk to the people you'd like to work with. Find out what they want, not just what you think they want, and how they would like to access it. It could be that your idea is exactly what they need, but they'd prefer a one-off session and not a series, or vice-versa. You can save a lot of time by asking and learning from the responses.

Include the market research in your timescales. Give yourself the opportunity to find out what's already available, how you will fit into the market, and the most effective way for you to do this.

As part of the research, you can also explore how people prefer to be contacted, where they hang out - literally, as in a geographical location, or on which social media platforms, through which charities, or if you're targeting professionals, which networking groups or national bodies they are all affiliated to.

Have a plan drawn out for this research. What questions do you need to have answered before you can move forward? What do you need to know? How will you communicate with the people who can answer these questions; meetings, phone calls, emails, Skype? Could you publish a survey and collect information that way? What is the current focus within the area in which you'd like to work, and how does your business fit with this?

One of the tried and tested methods of developing a business plan, having researched the market in which you'd like to operate, is the SWOT analysis which requires you to identify strengths, weaknesses, opportunities and threats:

You can use it to assess your own capabilities and areas for development, as well as using it to identify those of your competitors.

The **strengths** include the things you're brilliant at, and usually it's harder to fill in this section than the weaknesses one. Remember that nobody will see this! What resources do you have, and what sets you apart from your competitors, other than the dogs, who are obviously a huge strength and we're absolutely not biased.

The **weaknesses** include the areas that you don't know much about (yet) and the areas in which you might lack experience or expertise. These are only weaknesses at the moment, as once they have been identified they simply form part of the business plan. It doesn't mean you have to become an expert in this area, either. For example, hypothetically speaking, if there was a CIC whose Director had the accounting ability of a gnat, she might not choose to sign up for a course in money management but, instead, find a trusted and understanding accountant to ensure the weakness soon becomes a strength.

The **opportunities** include new business partnerships that could have emerged through your research, a gap in the market that only you can fill, a service that's opening in your geographical location; anything that could propel your business forwards.

The **threats** include any sudden changes in focus or agenda in the area in which you work. If you have one project with one target group, and the way in which engagement with that group changes, you could find your business at risk. If your research has found that there is direct competition, how will you approach this and how can you adapt what you're offering (if you need to) to ensure that you're getting work within the same sector?

Complete this analysis now, acknowledging where you are with your business today. You can only move forward from where you are right now. In a couple of months, do this again and see how much you've developed.

Strengths

Weaknesses

Opportunities

Threats

Business Plan

Please stay with us! This can be as exciting as you make it, honestly. If spreadsheets don't work for you, then paint your living room wall with a roadmap to success. As long as you can articulate what's going on for your business, do it in whatever way works. Be aware that if you're approaching a bank or a corporate business you might have to embrace a spreadsheet or two, but for now go with whatever approach will bring all of your ideas out of your head and into a structure that makes sense to you.

The business plan will help you to make sense of the finances, it will help you to set targets and apply timescales to those targets. It will enable you to prioritise, to define your actions and analyse how well you're doing against your targets. You're running a business now, it's not a hobby, so it's time to think and act in a way that helps you to make your CPPD business a roaring (or barking) success.

You can begin by thinking through these different areas; you will no doubt have more to add, and may find that some of these don't suit you. That's perfect, as it means you're thinking it through.

What's your CPPD business called? *Have you checked if this business name is available and also found out if your chosen website domain is available?*

What stage is your CPPD business at?

What is your CPPD business doing? *Can you remember your mission?!*

What do you need in order to start your CPPD business/move your CPPD business to the next stage?

What will you achieve with this CPPD business?

Who is involved with your CPPD business?

How are you going to manage your CPPD business?

Do you and/or your team need any training? *If yes, detail the training*

Explain your products and/or services.

What research have you done into where these products and/or services fit in the market?

Who is going to pay for this service and/or how will it be funded?

Who will you be working with?

How much will your products and/or services cost, and does this fit within the market you're working within?

Where will you be working and what costs are associated with this?

Will you be sub-contracting any work, and what are the costs associated with this?

Where will the dog(s) be coming from, and what are the cost implications?

Will you be stocking, developing and/or posting products, and what are the cost implications?

What is the legal status of your business?

Do you need any contracts, licenses, leases etc?

What is your budget, cash flow forecast, and how much money do you need to get started or move to the next level? *Ok, you might need to embrace a spreadsheet for this bit!*

What have we missed? What else do you need to consider?

You have the start of your business plan. Congratulations. If there are gaps, don't worry. If you had all of the answers at your fingertips, you wouldn't have picked up this book.

The money side of a social business is something to consider within the context of the legal structure you adopt. If you wrote down that you'll 'get funding', we urge you to go back and look at the finances! There is funding available, and if your business model relies on funding please plan accordingly and ensure your associated action planning includes not only the time you'll need to complete applications, but also the time you'll need to report back and account for what you've spent.

Have we missed anything? Oh, yes, actually running the business!

As a little tick box exercise, do you have:

O Premises - and a lease, or whatever else you might need to actually work there, which includes considering separate insurance if you're working at home.

O Insurance – having checked every aspect of the business from the laptop, to the car, to the liability and the dog(s)? Pet insurance doesn't cover taking your dog to work!

O Employment – have you got all of the information you need to ensure your team, in whatever context they're working, have the correct terms and conditions set up?

O A legal status set up, and have ensured that all of the rules and regulations within that status are adhered to?

O All of the financial side sorted out with regards to tax, book keeping, paying wages etc?

O Administration – have you checked you can operate under the business name, have a website and stationery ready to ensure professionalism and contact-ability?

O Do you have someone you can go to for help if there's something you're not sure about? This links to the advisory board, where having trusted legal help, accountancy help or specific business development can be invaluable.

What Do You Actually Do?

Back to that question! Now that you know what your CPPD business will look like, you've done the research and you know what will work, or you have a plan to find out what will work, you can start developing your sessions, your projects, your workshops, or all of those things.

What will you actually do?

Being able to show your funders, your partners and your clients your sessions plans, the aims and objectives, and the way in which you'll cover the agreed topics and how you will engage is what is going to turn your idea into reality. Saying you want to 'help' a specific group of people is a great start, it's the 'how' that is a little bit more difficult.

As you begin your planning, remember that as a social business you will be asked about your social impact. Measuring that social impact is worth thinking about from the start so that you can incorporate it into your plans. Having a measurement from the start is vital to show a baseline from which you have made a change through your CPPD business.

These measurements are important because:

You'll be able to see what is working and what might need to be changed in order to create the change you have committed to make.

You can see where the financial investment as well as the time and energy has gone, and whether it has brought about the results you aimed for.

In order to create interest amongst investors, you will have to make your social value as easy to understand as financial returns.

Since the Social Value Act has been passed, there is increased opportunity for social businesses to be commissioned if there is a clear method and understandable outcome within the tender.

Start looking at how you can measure success. How many people do you aim to engage with? How much time will you spend with those people? What are you aiming to change and how can this be measured (numerically, case studies, through external validation such as exams or work placements)? As this is a CPPD business, you also need to consider why the dog(s) make the difference. Could you do this without a dog? *No, of course not!* How will you evidence this?

Do you need external verification that your project does create social change? Could you commission a research project that can not only evidence the change you're making, but offer a professional review of what you're offering so that you can further develop your CPPD business?

The opportunities are endless. It's quite overwhelming, isn't it?

Well, if it was easy, everyone would be doing it. It's not easy, nothing worthwhile is easy. It is worth the effort though!

What next? What do you do now?

Firstly, take a deep breath and go and make a cuppa. You're about to begin the adventure of a lifetime, and every adventure needs a map. Wherever you are in your journey to CPPD business success, your map will need a big red paw print saying 'You are here'. Celebrate where you are now, as in a few months' time you'll look back and be able to see how far you've travelled.

Treat yourself to a fabulous new notebook, or open a new folder on your desktop which is not quite as inspiring, but time is of the essence. The world won't change itself! Go back through the notes you've made in this book and start to create an action plan. What are the different things you need to do, what gaps have you identified, who do you need to contact?

From there, start to prioritise. What needs to be done first, what can wait? What's a 'make or break' in terms of your next steps, and what is a 'nice to have' that can be left for a quiet evening when there's nothing on the TV.

Now you have your priorities, you can turn them into actions and set deadlines for each one. As you do this, you'll soon find out what is realistic for you. If you have ten priorities that all have to be completed by tomorrow, then make another cuppa and go back to the list.

Everything feels like a priority, yet part of running a successful CPPD business is being able to plan, work to deadlines, and stay healthy in the process. If you hit the wall nobody will be doing this for you, so go easy on yourself, take it step by step, and enjoy the process.

The most common phrase we hear from people is 'we want to do what you do'. When people say that, they're seeing the end result. They see us deliver a session with the help of exceptionally cute dogs. It is an honour and a privilege to be able to do that, and we're grateful to be living our dreams. The only reason we can deliver that session and live our dreams is due to the hours we've spent planning, getting insurance, doing our mileage, writing reports, getting them wrong, writing them again, and having lists about lists of what we need to do next. That process continues as you're reading this.

It's oh so glamorous!

Thank you for reading our words, for wanting to make a difference and for taking the time to develop your CPPD business for the people who need it. You have work to do now, and it will absolutely be worth the time and effort. Good Luck!

Business Name:	The K9 Project
Business Website:	www.thek9project.co.uk
Business Facebook:	www.facebook.com/thek9project
Business Twitter:	@TheK9Project
Geographical Location:	Cambridgeshire
Please describe your business:	Canine Partnership Education, Learning and Personal Development for children and young people. Coaching, workshops and mentoring for professionals
What structure is your business registered as and why did you choose this structure:	I have tried a few! They all worked at different points. Initially, I started a business partnership with my husband who I started the project with. Why? It was easy, straightforward and simple to manage from all angles. We then took the decision to be a non-profit; a company limited by guarantee. Why? It was the simplest way to be able to apply for some charitable funding, to maintain control of day to day activities, to ensure speed of decision making, and to be able to earn money while not working to a 'committee'. Now I operate as a sole trader. Why? After 6 years of running a non-profit and increasing our range of programmes as well as our staff group, I became disillusioned with the funding systems and government approach to distribution of funds. I made the decision to streamline and refocus on what I set out to do initially without engaging in the funding process.
How do dogs feature	My dogs work in partnership on all aspects

in your business:	of the business; working alongside myself and children and young people. I use dogs' natural behaviours to provide opportunities for growth and development.
Do you have paid staff and / or volunteers within your team:	At one stage when we operated as a limited company I had 4 sessional staff and 10 volunteers. Now I work alone.
What is the number one challenge you face in running a social business / social enterprise?	Maintaining a level of work that is enough to pay the mortgage, consistently across the whole year.
What three things do you wish you'd known when you started your venture:	I've quite enjoyed the journey of discovery exactly as it has been. However, if I had to pick a few it would be that the people who show the most enthusiasm for the venture are not the people who write the cheques! A greater knowledge about funding streams and how hard it can be to get 'in' with certain grant givers would have also been handy.
What would you change in your business if you could?	Nothing.
What piece of advice would you like to offer someone who is starting their journey in this area of work:	Think about and plan what you are going to do, but don't let the process overtake action! Keep laughing, don't take it all personally, stay well and healthy in yourself. Love your dog(s). Keep both of you safe. Find people to support you.

Business Name:	Canine Perspective CIC
Business Website:	www.canine-perspective.com
Business Facebook:	www.facebook.com/TeamCanineP/
Business Twitter:	@TeamCanineP
Geographical Location:	South Wales
Please describe your business:	We're a social enterprise inspiring positive change using the power of the human-canine bond. We work in four distinct areas; offering dog training and behaviour sessions, personal development & team building workshops for humans, a product line, and our series of social projects.
What structure is your business registered as and why did you choose this structure:	We're a Community Interest Company (CIC), limited by guarantee, which is one of the recognised structures used to register a 'social enterprise'. A CIC gives us scope to grow while ensuring we have terms of reference that maintain our social mission and purpose. We have two Directors and an Advisory Board, so we keep bureaucracy to a minimum.
How do dogs feature in your business:	It was one of our dogs that started this business! A book called *Reggie & Me*, written by Marie, has been successful in sharing the power of the human-canine bond through the story of teenage rape survivor and her rescue dog, Reggie. This social enterprise began with a desire to bring the book to life, and our signature social project for survivors, Canine Hope, does just that. We have a combination of approaches throughout the different areas

	of our business, working with clients' dogs, our own dogs and rescue dogs.
Do you have paid staff and / or volunteers within your team:	We took the decision at the beginning of our venture that employees wouldn't be part of the plan for us. We have specific roles outsourced to professionals (accounting, for example!) and use freelance professionals where appropriate. This is something that's reviewed regularly as the business grows. Never say never!
What is the number one challenge you face in running a social business / social enterprise?	The challenge for me (Marie) used to be that I didn't really know anyone else who was doing this. I don't mean the dog stuff necessarily, but people who had taken a risk and leapt into the world of social enterprise. Being accepted into the School of Social Enterprise was a game changer in that respect, as I met incredible people who were just like me; taking a risk, learning as they went along, and putting their heart and soul into following their passion. Being around social entrepreneurs who are truly making a difference in the world is inspiring and they understand the journey in a way not many other people do. Find some people who inspire you and learn from them.
What three things do you wish you'd known when you started your venture:	1. I was told hundreds of times that a business isn't built in a few weeks. *I didn't listen!* It does take time, and I hadn't factored a lot of the intricacies into the early plans. That soon changedand I have now

	adopted the five-p's approach: Preparation Prevents Piss Poor Performance.
	2. Done is better than perfect!
	3. That it's ok to change the direction of your business and ditch the things you don't like doing. It frees up your time and energy for the elements you love, and that's where you're much more likely to succeed.
What would you change in your business if you could?	Nothing, we're enjoying the ride.
What piece of advice would you like to offer someone who is starting their journey in this area of work:	That there's no right or wrong and everything is a learning opportunity. You'll mess things up and that's ok, it's part of the adventure. Celebrate the good times and don't aim to do things perfectly, aim to do things brilliantly! It's your business and your rules, so do it your way as that's what will make the difference.

Business Name:	People & Animals UK C.I.C.
Business Website:	www.peopleandanimals.org.uk
Business Facebook:	https://www.facebook.com/AAIUK
Business Twitter:	https://twitter.com/UKPeopleAnimals
Geographical Location:	Nationwide
Please describe your business:	People and Animals UK is a Community Interest Company (C.I.C.) dedicated to promoting therapeutic interaction between people and animals by; - Creating opportunities for like-minded individuals to share and promote standards of best practice in Animal-Assisted Intervention (AAI) and Animal-Assisted Therapy (AAT) through networking events and themed workshops. - Collaboration with individuals and organisations across both the human and animal sector, to deliver sound training courses for those interested in exploring the human-animal bond in greater depth. - Delivery of Animal-Assisted Intervention (AAI) and Equine Assisted Learning (EAL) programmes, incorporating mutually beneficial human-animal relationships, into communities throughout the UK. - Multi-agency working to promote safe relationships between pets and families.
What structure is	We chose to establish People & Animals UK

your business registered as and why did you choose this structure:	as a Community Interest Company (C.I.C.) as it was the best fit for us, being a small start-up organisation it was relatively straight forward and inexpensive to set up and provides us with the appropriate level of flexibility.
How do dogs feature in your business:	Dog visiting programmes, on 121 and group levels across target groups, providing; - therapeutic intervention when working alongside healthcare professionals - assisted educational opportunities - community resilience and cohesion - fundraising opportunities and community events - practitioner training
Do you have paid staff and / or volunteers within your team:	We have 2 members of paid staff and a team of volunteers.
What is the number one challenge you face in running a social business / social enterprise?	The level of 'invisible legwork' required by practitioners to ensure programmes and services are delivered effectively.
What three things do you wish you'd known when you started your venture:	1. Have belief in your abilities 2. Know when to say 'no' 3. Be mindful of your work-life balance at all times!
What would you change in your business if you could?	Nothing actually, it is a learning journey and all aspects are valuable.
What piece of	Try it, you don't know where it may lead.

advice would you like to offer someone who is starting their journey in this area of work:	Be open to help along the way.

Business Name:	PET RESPECT
Business Website:	www.petrespect.org.uk
Business Facebook:	Pet Respect
Business Twitter:	@PetRespect
Geographical Location:	Hull East Riding of Yorkshire
Please describe your business:	Pet Respect delivers educational workshops to school children. Our workshops are 'Animals Feelings and Needs', 'Animals Role In War' and an Anti Bullying presentation. We also offer Animal Assisted Therapy-AAT to smaller groups where we tailor sessions to suit the needs of the child or young person. The children have various problems and social issues. We use the therapy dogs to help improve their self-esteem and wellbeing.
What structure is your business registered as and why did you choose this structure:	Charity and Public Limited Company Charity so that we could fundraise and apply for grants. PLC as we were advised to be a company before becoming a charity.
How do dogs feature in your business:	Dogs feature all the time in Pet respect. They are our 'tools' to educate children about respect for all living beings. Our therapy dogs are extremely popular with school children; we have received excellent feedback from teachers and the children. Teachers report an improvement in behaviour when the children work with the dogs.
Do you have paid staff and / or volunteers within your team:	Pet Respect has 10 volunteers. Three of them sometimes get sessional tutors fees, depending on funding.
What is the number one	Getting paid for our work (which we

challenge you face in running a social business / social enterprise?	finally are!!) We had to prove ourselves first and gain a good reputation.
What do you wish you'd known when you started your venture:	1) What to charge for our services as there is no-one offering AAT in the area 2) How difficult it is for people to understand the benefits of AAT
What would you change in your business if you could?	We wish we could be stronger and learn to say 'NO' more often.
What piece of advice would you like to offer someone who is starting their journey in this area of work:	Learn to walk before you run. In other words, perfect one thing before you move onto the next. It has taken us nearly 8 years to get to where we wanted to be.

Business Name:	HumAnima CIC
Business Website:	www.humanima.co.uk
Business Facebook:	www.facebook.com/HumAnimaCIC
Business Twitter:	@HumAnimaCIC
Geographical Location:	Wolverhampton
Please describe your business:	HumAnima CIC is a Wolverhampton based social enterprise offering personal, professional and holistic support through Counselling, Animal Assisted Therapy and training.
What structure is your business registered as and why did you choose this structure:	HumAnima CIC is a Community Interest Company which is a social enterprise form. This was chosen to provide the most benefit to its stakeholders along with transparency whilst providing the Director with a realistic income.
How do dogs feature in your business:	I work with my English Cocker Spaniel, Flossie who is a trained and temperament assessed Therapy dog. She works with me in my Counselling practice with clients who wish to have her present but she also joins me on visits to different establishments where we provide Animal Assisted Activities (AAA) and Animal Assisted Therapy (AAT). Flossie is a key team player in the business but is approaching retirement now that she is 9yrs old. We will be looking for a new Therapy Dog who can

	learn the ropes soon.
	I also teach students on our Animal Assisted Therapy in Counselling course what they need to consider when choosing a Therapy Animal – invariably these are dogs although there are some more unusual animals that students have chosen to work with. I also teach students about Therapy Animal suitability including temperament, breed, history, rescue & gender considerations.
Do you have paid staff and / or volunteers within your team:	The Director is paid but we also have 2 volunteer non-executive Directors. We will be looking to bring volunteers on board to help with the running and development of the organisation.
What is the number one challenge you face in running a social business / social enterprise?	Doing everything myself – it is incredibly difficult deciding how to delegate and what to delegate to other people the best way possible. It is also very difficult establishing a work-life balance especially when you work from home.
What three things do you wish you'd known when you started your venture:	1. No one will tell you what to do – you have to tell yourself. – This may seem obvious, as you are "your own boss" but those who have only ever worked for others will recognise this can be a difficult transition when you don't know what you don't know and those

	things need doing!
	2. It can be a very lonely existence – surround yourself with supportive networks whether those are family, professional or friends. You will need them!
	3. You need to create your own work-life balance and structure. Weekends no longer feel like weekends but another day when you COULD be working. The line between work and life becomes very thin and often indistinguishable so think about how you will make that more defined.
What would you change in your business if you could?	I would have more help – it's difficult to know who and how to share what is essentially your "baby". It is difficult to let up the reigns and hand over to others but it is essential especially when life challenges and changes happen.
What piece of advice would you like to offer someone who is starting their journey in this area of work:	Remember how you can celebrate the small things. No one will be there to pat you on the back except you. How will you recognise your wins and celebrate those? Who will appreciate the magnitude of your small wins?

Business Name:	Dogs Helping Kids
Business Website:	www.dogshelpingkids.co.uk
Business Facebook:	www.facebook.com/dogshelpingkids
Geographical Location:	North Devon (where HQ is), but work across England (from York down to Cornwall and into Wales).
Please describe your business:	We train carefully selected dogs as both educational and therapeutic aids to work with and help children and teenagers (aged between 6 – 18) in school, colleges and libraries. Our DHK School Dogs teach children non-violence, empathy, respect, kindness, love, responsibility, friendship and trust. It takes 3 years of dog training with the charity and passing 6 increasingly difficult assessments for a dog to certify as a DHK School Dog, and then each year they are annually assessed in their place of work. The impact our DHK School Dogs have on both children and teenagers is life changing and has made an impact where all other therapies have failed. Our DHK School Dogs have improved academic achievement, increased literacy skills, calmed behaviour down, increased social skills and self-esteem, increased confidence, taught responsibility and respect to all life, helped prevent truancy, and motivated children who were not that attentive. Our DHK School Dogs work in mainstream schools, behavioural schools, special needs schools, colleges and private schools. DHK – Changing lives, one child at a time.

What structure is your business registered as and why did you choose this structure:	Registered National Charity 1148913 To be able to raise funds and to be able to apply for funds to enable the work with our dogs to continue into the future. I also felt it was the best route for DHK to go down after seeking legal advice and chatting to loads and loads of charities!
How do dogs feature in your business:	Dogs are at the heart of our charity – each DHK School Dog is literally gold dust and without our dogs we would not exist – they are the charity! The welfare of our School Dogs is of the highest priority to DHK. We teach all DHK School Dog owners how to recognise stress in dogs and they must all have an excellent understanding of canine body language.
Do you have paid staff and / or volunteers within your team:	I am paid (below minimum wage sadly) – there are a couple of awesome volunteers who help with some of the running of the charity. The remainder of the volunteers are the owners of the School Dogs.
What is the number one challenge you face in running a social business / social enterprise?	Not receiving enough local support with regards to funding or volunteers – sadly we have 3 huge local charities and smaller charities like DHK do not get a look in. Also, we find it hard to secure funding as a national charity – this is such a difficult and ongoing task with no let up!
What three things do you wish you'd known when you started your venture:	1. How hard it is to run a charity! 2. How hard it is to find funding or people/businesses willing to help/assist /support 3. How to fill out grant forms in the best way to achieve funding

What would you change in your business if you could?	Not having an email address – I run the charity 24-7 and it is a very gruelling daily task from training the dogs to running workshops, from meetings to visiting schools and college all over the country. I receive hundreds of emails each week and this is a full-time job in itself. People want an answer straight away (due to social media) and they do not realise we are a small charity and it is me who is answering the emails, and there are some days I simply cannot get to answering them!
What piece of advice would you like to offer someone who is starting their journey in this area of work:	No matter how many knock backs you get (or if someone tells you you're crazy for thinking 'that will work'!) you must, must keep going and work really hard – Animal Assisted Therapy and working with dogs is such a rewarding job to do with often amazing outcomes - gain experience from those who are already running something similar to what you are hoping to undertake. If you are going to work with dogs in AAT, it is really important to understand all about dog training (positive / force free), dog behaviour, stress in dogs and dog welfare – you must become a doggy expert!

#0397 - 270317 - C0 - 210/148/6 - PB - DID1795210